PLANT-TASTIC!
WHOA!
FREAKY PLANT FACTS

BY REX RUBY

BEARPORT PUBLISHING

Minneapolis, Minnesota

Credits

Cover and title page, © Jason Bazzano/Alamy; 4–5, © Drew Angerer/Getty Images and © amedved/iStock; 6–7, © Ziga Plahutar/iStock; 8–9, © Jess Kraft/Shutterstock; 10, © Damian Pawlos/iStock; 11, © hlsnow/iStock; 12, © Scenic Corner/Adobe Stock; 13, © Cristi/Adobe Stock; 14–15, © Ryan Green/iStock; 16, © Sergii_Trofymchuk/iStock; 17, © passion4nature/iStock; 18–19, © James W. Thompson/Shutterstock; 19, © Erin Paul Donovan/Alamy; 20–21, © Fabian Plock/Alamy; 22, © Artjom Kissler/iStock; and 23, © amedved/iStock.

Bearport Publishing Company Product Development Team
President: Jen Jenson; Director of Product Development: Spencer Brinker; Managing Editor: Allison Juda; Associate Editor: Naomi Reich; Senior Designer: Colin O'Dea; Associate Designer: Elena Klinkner; Associate Designer: Kayla Eggert; Product Development Specialist: Anita Stasson

Library of Congress Cataloging-in-Publication Data

Names: Ruby, Rex, author.
Title: Whoa! : freaky plant facts / by Rex Ruby.
Description: Minneapolis, Minnesota : Bearport Publishing Company, [2024] | Series: Plant-tastic! | Includes bibliographical references and index.
Identifiers: LCCN 2022058244 (print) | LCCN 2022058245 (ebook) | ISBN 9798888220429 (library binding) | ISBN 9798888222355 (paperback) | ISBN 9798888223574 (ebook)
Subjects: LCSH: Plants--Juvenile literature. | Plants--Juvenile literature.
Classification: LCC QK49 .R83 2024 (print) | LCC QK49 (ebook) | DDC 581--dc23/eng/20221215
LC record available at https://lccn.loc.gov/2022058244
LC ebook record available at https://lccn.loc.gov/2022058245

Copyright © 2024 Bearport Publishing Company. All rights reserved. No part of this publication may be reproduced in whole or in part, stored in any retrieval system, or transmitted in any form or by any means, electronic, mechanical, photocopying, recording, or otherwise, without written permission from the publisher.

For more information, write to Bearport Publishing, 5357 Penn Avenue South, Minneapolis, MN 55419.

CONTENTS

What Is That Terrible Smell?.......... 4
Small, Tall, and Unusual............. 6
A Giant Tree Trunk 8
The Oldest Trees 10
Giant Pine Cones 12
Is It a Leaf or a Boat? 14
The Smallest Flowers............... 16
A Ghostly Plant................... 18
Not Much to Look At 20

Science Lab......................... 22
Glossary............................ 23
Index 24
Read More.......................... 24
Learn More Online................... 24
About the Author.................... 24

WHAT IS THAT TERRIBLE SMELL?

Crowds have gathered to see one of the biggest flowers on Earth. The titan arum flower can grow to be 10 feet (3 m) tall. *Whoa!* But what is that awful stink? Is it rotten meat or animal poop? Neither! The smell is coming from the big flower.

It can take a titan arum plant over seven years to make a new flower. It **blooms** for only about two days.

SMALL, TALL, AND UNUSUAL

Nearly half a million types of plants grow on Earth. They can come in many different shapes and sizes, from tiny moss to towering redwoods. Luckily, most don't smell like the titan arum, but they may be equally unusual in other ways. Whether big or small, stinky or sweet, this planet has some pretty freaky plants.

Most moss grows only a few centimeters high, while some redwood trees tower hundreds of feet tall.

A GIANT TREE TRUNK

Almost 2,000 years ago, a cypress tree known as the Tule (TOO-lee) tree began to grow. Each year its **trunk** got bigger and bigger. Now, the trunk is more than 150 ft (45 m) around—and it's still growing! This is one of the biggest tree trunks on Earth.

Although the Tule tree may look like the trunks of many trees stuck together, it's only one plant.

8

The Tule tree is in Mexico.

THE OLDEST TREES

The Tule tree is old, but it's not the most ancient tree on Earth. That record belongs to a bristlecone pine that is almost 5,000 years old. How do we know a tree's age? Every year, a tree grows new wood under its bark. This forms rings in the trunk. If a scientist were to **slice** a tree's trunk, they could count these rings of growth.

Scientists can also use a special tool to cut out a small piece of trunk and count a tree's rings without harming the plant.

The location of the oldest bristlecone pine is kept secret to keep the tree safe.

GIANT PINE CONES

Pine trees grow cones with spiky **scales** to hold their seeds. Once the seeds are fully grown, the scales open and the seeds fall to the ground. Some cones are small but others can be huge. The sugar pine tree's cones can grow up to 2 ft (60 cm) long!

A coulter pine cone is both large and heavy. It can weigh as much as a large watermelon.

A coulter pine tree cone

A sugar pine tree cone

13

IS IT A LEAF OR A BOAT?

It's not just trees or cones that can be huge—leaves can, too! Giant water lily leaves can grow to be about 10 ft (3 m) wide. Despite their massive size, they still float. How do they do it? The bottom of each leaf has many small ribs that trap air to help keep it above water.

The biggest water lily leaves can hold the weight of an average adult!

THE SMALLEST FLOWERS

Not all freaky plants are giant. Tiny duckweed are the smallest flowering plants on Earth. It would take more than 5,000 of them to fill the inside of a small bottle cap. The flowers of the floating duckweed are so small that they can be seen only when viewed under a **microscope**.

Duckweed float on water. They move to new places on the feet and feathers of birds that swim through them.

A GHOSTLY PLANT

Most plants are green because of the **chlorophyll** (KLOR-uh-fil) found inside them. This substance helps plants use sunlight to make food. However, ghost pipe plants are often all white. They don't have any chlorophyll, and they don't need sunshine to live or grow. Ghost pipe plants survive in dark forests by stealing **nutrients** from other plants nearby.

Ghost pipe plants turn black when they die.

19

NOT MUCH TO LOOK AT

Tree tumbos look like dead, messy piles of leaves. But these desert plants are alive and can be more than 1,000 years old. In all that time, they grow only two leaves that can each be more than 20 ft (6 m) long! Earth is home to many plants. But whether they are really old, huge, tiny, or even stinky—freaky plants are everywhere.

Over time, the tumbo's two leaves get torn and tangled together in the wind.

SCIENCE LAB
PLANT TREASURE HUNT

Go on a plant treasure hunt to discover what's growing in your backyard or a park. Look with your eyes, and see if you can find . . .

- A leaf that is bigger than your hand
- A flower smaller than your fingernail
- A tree with a thick trunk
- A tree with a strange shape
- A plant that has a smell
- A pine cone
- An amazing or unusual plant

GLOSSARY

blooms opens as a flower

chlorophyll the substance in plants that traps sunlight and gives the plants their green color

microscope a tool scientists use to see very small things

nutrients substances plants need to grow and be healthy

scales small, overlapping pieces that form a hard shell

slice to cut a thin, flat piece of something

trunk the main woody stem of a tree

INDEX

desert 20
duckweed 16–17
flowers 4–5, 16, 22
ghost pipe 18–19
giant water lily 14–15
leaves 14–15, 20–22
pine cones 12–14, 22
rings 10
titan arum 4–6
tree tumbo 20–21
trunks 8, 10, 22
Tule tree 8–10

READ MORE

Finan, Catherine C. *Plants (X-treme Facts: Science).* Minneapolis: Bearport Publishing Company, 2021.

Kaner, Etta. *Pretty Tricky: The Sneaky Ways Plants Survive.* Toronto, ON: Owlkids Books, 2020.

Loh-Hagan, Virginia. *Weird Science: Plants and Fungi (How the Heck Does That Work?!).* Ann Arbor, MI: Cherry Lake Publishing, 2021.

LEARN MORE ONLINE

1. Go to **www.factsurfer.com** or scan the QR code below.
2. Enter "**Whoa**" into the search box.
3. Click on the cover of this book to see a list of websites.

ABOUT THE AUTHOR

Rex Ruby lives in Minnesota with his family. If he were a plant, he'd be very large but hopefully not smelly.

24